SHORTCUT TO PERIL

SHORTCUT TO PERIL

James I. Clark

Illustrated by Marc Glessner

RAINTREE PUBLISHERS
Milwaukee • Toronto • Melbourne • London

Library of Congress Number: 79-22151

1 2 3 4 5 6 7 8 9 0 84 83 82 81 80

Printed and bound in the United States of America.

Library of Congress Cataloging in Publication Data

Clark, James I.
  Shortcut to Peril.

  SUMMARY: Relates the adventure of a beaver trapper who survived for 57 days after becoming lost in the wilderness of British Columbia.
  1. Wilderness survival — British Columbia — Juvenile literature. 2. Woodcock, Ronald — Juvenile literature. 3. Fur traders — Canada — Biography — Juvenile literature. [1. Wilderness survival. 2. Survival] I. Glessner, Marc. II. Title.
GV200.5.C56   613.6'9'09711   79-22151
ISBN 0-8172-1570-0 lib. bdg.

CONTENTS

CHAPTER 1

Wiped Out

A fire drove Ron Woodcock out into the wilderness. The wilderness almost killed him.

The little town of Endako, where Ron Woodcock lived, is in northwestern British Columbia, Canada. It lies about 160 miles west of Prince George, a city of around 10,000 people. The town rests on the north bank of the Endako River, near where it flows into Lake Fraser. Woodcock and his wife and six children made up about one-eighth of Endako's population of sixty people.

During the winter in that northern land, the temperature falls far below zero. Snow lies heavy on the ground. And that one February night in 1971 was really cold. The Woodcock children huddled together to keep warm.

Suddenly, in the middle of the night, the smell of smoke awakened Ron. He leaped out of bed and ran to the bedroom door. What he saw

frightened him. The whole kitchen was in flames!

Ron Woodcock never knew how the fire started. Certainly right then he didn't stop to try to figure it out. He yelled to awaken his wife and six children. Then, grabbing a bunch of blankets, he led them out into the clear, cold night.

Endako was too small to have a fire department. Even a bucket brigade wouldn't have worked. The river was frozen. The fierce flames soon ate through the entire house. Ron and his family could only watch it burn. Ron's brother took the Woodcocks in for the rest of the night.

Only in the morning did Ron really understand what had happened. "We've been wiped out," he said to his wife. All their belongings lay in ashes. They had only a little money. Ron worked for the railroad, but that didn't pay much. There were few other jobs in that wilderness country. What was he to do?

The Woodcocks found a house to rent in Endako. They scratched up some furniture. But the future looked bleak.

Ron and his wife talked it over. "There's only one thing left," he finally said. He could go into the wilderness for a few weeks and trap beaver. He had lived in the wilderness before. He knew how to take care of himself. And beaver skins were bringing about $20 apiece. If he could come back with, say, 100 skins, they might have enough to start building another house. So Ron and his wife agreed: he would do it.

The next day, Ron talked with his boss on the railroad. The man agreed that Ron could take a few weeks off and then come back to his job. With that, Ron waited for spring.

As the weather warmed, Ron rounded up some beaver traps. He laid out his wilderness equipment—his rifle, ammunition, hunting knife, compass, an ax, his sleeping bag, matches, and a backpack. His wife packed some dried meat and some rice for him. Ron planned to get food as he went. With his rifle, he could have rabbit,

woodchuck, maybe even moose to eat. And as spring wore on, there would be wild berries.

Next, Ron talked with Bill Jenkins, a bush pilot. In his small plane Jenkins flew people to places where there were no roads or railroads. The plane had floats instead of wheels so it could land on water. Jenkins agreed to fly Ron into the wilderness when the ice cleared.

The day they left in April dawned clear and cool. Snow still lay deep in the mountains, but ice on the Endako River and Lake Fraser had broken up. Wild flowers were beginning to bud. Soon they would burst into bright colors.

Early that morning, Bill Jenkins and Ron with his equipment climbed into the plane. Jenkins gunned the engine and they took off. As the plane climbed, Jenkins slowly turned toward the northwest. They headed for Lake Damochax, about 200 miles away. Damochax is a small lake. It doesn't show on many maps of British Columbia.

In less than two hours Ron and Jenkins spotted Lake Damochax. Jenkins eased the plane's nose downward. Then, circling the lake, he cut the power and set the plane down gently on the water. He taxied toward shore.

In shallow water, Ron unloaded his equipment and carried it to land. "See you right here in eight weeks!" Jenkins shouted as he started the engine.

Ron nodded and waved. Jenkins swung the plane around, headed it into the wind, and took off. The plane climbed smoothly into the almost cloudless sky.

Ron carried his equipment to the empty cabin on the shore of Lake Damochax. The cabin would be his base for trapping. At the door, he looked around. His eyes took in the calm lake, the trees, along its shore, and snow-capped mountains in the far distance. To him it was a lovely sight. He had often thought of how nice it would be if he could have his family with him there and spend the rest of his life in the wilderness. "You're at peace," he had said to himself. "You're your own

boss. Fish and game are plentiful. You're in a world you're making for yourself, and no other world exists." Well, he thought, I'll have eight weeks of it anyway. Then I'll be home with a string of beaver skins and the Woodcocks' troubles would be over.

Eight weeks. Many more than eight weeks would pass before Ron Woodcock would see another human being.

CHAPTER 2

Lost

"Busy as a beaver" is certainly true about beavers. These furry creatures with large buck teeth seem never to rest. They seem always to be cutting down trees, dragging logs and branches and sticks, carrying mud on their long flat tails, and swimming. Now and then they take time off to eat, and one of their favorite foods is the bark of the aspen tree. When they have nothing else to do, beavers play.

Beavers live in ponds, small lakes, and streams. They are powerful swimmers. They use their broad, flat tails as flippers to move them through the water. And they can stay under water for a long time. Beavers also use their tails to signal danger to each other. They slap the tails against the water. This makes a loud, popping noise.

When beavers take over a stream, they build a dam. Swiftly their long sharp teeth gnaw through good-sized trees to topple them to the ground.

Sometimes they cut the log into smaller pieces. They snip off branches.

After they have gathered material, beavers drag logs into the stream and pull them down to the bottom. There they fix the logs in the mud. Gradually, with logs, branches, and sticks, they build their dam. Finally, the top of the dam rises above the surface. The water behind the dam grows quiet.

Now beavers are ready to build their houses, called lodges. Again they use logs, sticks, and branches, and bark as well. As they build upward from the bottom of the stream, they leave space for rooms and passageways. When the lodge is high enough above the surface to suit them, the

beavers cover it with mud, which they carry on their tails as they swim. After they have slapped enough mud over the top of the lodge, they pile a few small logs and some branches over it. A beaver lodge looks messy—with logs, sticks, branches, and mud piled helter-skelter in the water. But for beavers it makes a cozy home.

Once there were millions of beavers in North America. But people trapped them and sold the skins. Hats made of soft beaver fur were very popular. So were beaver coats.

Today, most of the beaver are gone. Coats are still made of beaver fur, though, and most of the beaver that remain are found in northern Canada. That is where, in the spring of 1971, Ron Woodcock set out to find them.

Ron had no trouble. He found many beaver lodges along streams and ponds. He set his traps near them. Soon Ron's line of traps strung out for many miles. He traveled some of the route each day. He took out the beavers he had caught and set the traps again.

After three weeks had passed, Ron had fifty skins. Great! he thought. By the end of eight weeks I should easily have twice that many. Ron was glad he had gone into the wilderness. It was really paying off. Soon things would be fine for the Woodcock family once again.

On May 31 Ron left his cabin. He was going about twenty miles up Slowmaldo Creek. He would pick up some skins he had stored there. On that day he wore a light jacket, a wool shirt, and rubber boots. In his backpack he carried his sleeping bag, food, his ax and rifle, and fifteen bullets. The backpack weighed about thirty pounds.

Moving up Slowmaldo Creek, Ron came to Groundhog Pass, a narrow stretch between high hills. Working his way through the underbrush that lined the pass, he found his skins.

During the next few days, Ron kept busy cleaning the skins. Then he lashed half of them together in a bundle that weighed about sixty pounds. That, plus his backpack, made a heavy load. So Ron decided to find a shortcut back to Slowmaldo Creek. He had a three days' supply of food.

Ron headed south. After six hours of tramping through high underbrush, he came upon a creek. He could see several beaver dams strung across it. But these puzzled Ron. He knew he had never

seen those dams before. Looking around, he could see mountains in the distance. But he had never seen them before either.

He sat down on a fallen log. All was quiet: the small stream, trees here and there, underbrush, mountains in the distance. Gradually something dawned on him, and he began to feel a little sick to his stomach. Ron Woodcock was lost. He pulled his small notebook and pencil from his pocket and wrote down the date: June 5, 1971.

CHAPTER 3

A Moose and a Grizzly

The sun was setting. Ron remained on the log, thinking. Was Slowmaldo Creek east or west? He had no way to know. Should he go back to Groundhog Pass and start over? There was no trail to follow. He might miss the pass entirely.

Perhaps, he thought, this little stream he sat beside might lead to some place he would know. He might follow it south. And somewhere to the south lay the town of Hazelton. His mother lived there. But, he figured, Hazelton was a long way off—probably more than a hundred miles. And that was in a straight line, as an airplane flies. Ron knew that it would be impossible for him to travel there in a straight line. He had no idea how many miles he might have to cover.

Yet Ron had to decide, and he did. He would follow the creek. The next day, pulling on his backpack and the heavy load of skins, he set out.

He could not travel fast. Every step was hard

work. There was no trail along the creek. Ron had to work his way through rough and tangled brush and small trees. To get around some places, he had to move away from the creek. This meant he had to go up and down hills. This was especially hard with the load he carried. Often he came across windfalls—dead trees the wind had blown down. In some places windfalls were piled twenty-five feet high. Ron had to go around them, through more dense underbrush. His load seemed heavier and heavier. Two days passed.

At the end of the second day, Ron had to make another decision. This was the hardest one of all. The beaver skins were just too heavy. He could no longer carry them. He would have to leave them behind.

This was a crushing blow. Those skins and the others he had gathered were the whole reason for being in the wilderness. Without them he would have just wasted his time. All his work would be for nothing. His family would be no better off. In fact, everyone would be worse off. Ron could have been earning some money working for the railroad during all that time. That fire in February had wiped the family out. Now, with Ron lost and having to fight hard to reach help without his skins, the Woodcocks would stay wiped out.

But the picture had changed. Those fifty skins

faded from Ron's mind. He was no longer a trapper gathering beaver to sell for $20 each. He was lost, and in a fight for his life. He had no idea what lay ahead or how long the fight would last.

Some persons grow terribly frightened when they're lost. They panic. They set out in any direction, just to be doing something. Some, after a time, find that they have traveled in a circle. They become exhausted and lose hope. They die.

That will not happen to me, Ron thought. I've lived in the wilderness before. I know enough to

stay calm and think carefully. Go easy. Don't wear yourself out. I'll live, he said to himself. I'll get home again. It doesn't matter how long it takes. I know I'll make it.

Ron's body was tough. He weighed 170 pounds, and he was mostly muscle and bones. He was sure that his body would see him through.

Grimly, as the sun set that afternoon, Ron Woodcock cooked a handful of rice. He ate only that. He couldn't tell whether there would be game to hunt. He had to make the little food he had last as long as possible.

Darkness fell. And as Ron zipped himself into his sleeping bag beside the dying fire, he said goodbye to his beaver skins. He thought only of survival.

Shortly after dawn the next day, Ron set out again. The going was easier now without the heavy bundle of skins.

Each day Ron plodded for twelve or thirteen hours. He stopped when he grew tired. He did not wear himself out. One day he brought down both a woodchuck and a grouse. That evening he feasted, but he saved some of the meat. He knew he might not see more game for days.

On the evening of the tenth day, Ron made camp on the bank of the stream he had been following. He glanced downstream. What he saw made his heart skip a beat. A huge moose was walking slowly toward the water.

There, Ron told himself, was enough food to last for many days. The moose was about fifty yards away. The breeze was blowing from the animal toward Ron. The moose could not smell Ron's presence.

Carefully, Ron edged toward his rifle. He felt for it, not taking his eyes off the moose. He picked up the gun as the thirsty animal stopped at the water's edge. It looked around. Seeing no danger, and smelling none, it shook its huge antlers. And then it lowered its long nose into the stream to suck up water. Ron steadied his rifle, squinting down the sights. He held his breath and fired.

The moose never heard the sound. Its front legs buckled and it went down.

Dropping his rifle, Ron ran toward the animal, pulling out his hunting knife. He quickly slit the moose's throat to bleed it well. Then, pulling hard, he dragged it away from the stream.

Now he was tired, dead tired. He would have to wait until the next day to do more. Ron returned to his camp.

As he slid into his sleeping bag that night, Ron hoped there were no grizzly bears or wolves around. That moose was his. It meant that he could survive a little longer.

Ten days had passed. How many more? he wondered as he drifted off to sleep.

The next day, with his knife and ax, Ron removed a hindquarter from the moose. He carried it to where he was camped. He skinned it and spent the whole day cooking the meat. Carefully he packed away about twenty pounds of it. He saved a choice bit, and at the end of the day he began cooking it for his supper.

As the meat sizzled over the fire, Ron looked toward where the moose carcass lay. The sun was low on his right. The view was hazy. He saw a huge shadow move out of the trees and toward the carcass. And then Ron made out what it was—a grizzly bear, the largest and most fearsome creature in North America. Ron froze. His eyes were riveted on the animal.

Ron had all the meat he could carry. He didn't care if the bear enjoyed a feast. But what then? What might happen after dark? The breeze still drifted from the carcass toward Ron. But what if, later, the grizzly circled around and suddenly smelled a human, asleep by the fire?

In late spring, bears are not long out of their winter's hibernation. Their weight is down. Much of the time they're hungry. They're touchy. No one can tell just how a grizzly will act at any time, but especially in the spring.

A grizzly might pay little attention to a human. Or it might attack without warning, in daylight or

at night. Few people have survived a grizzly's sharp, ripping fangs and slashing claws. Its scientific name is *ursa horribilis*. And to anyone faced with the angry power of a huge, blackish brown wild body weighing as much as a thousand pounds, the sight is horrible indeed.

The bear smelled no danger. It didn't know it was being watched. Reaching the carcass, the grizzly reared up on its hind legs, sniffing the wind and looking around. It stretched at least nine feet tall. Had it seen the man, crouched hardly a stone's throw away?

Seeing nothing and smelling nothing, the grizzly dropped back on all fours. It grabbed the moose carcass in its powerful jaws and began to drag it toward the trees along the stream bank. As it did so, it moved closer to Ron.

About 100 feet from Ron, the bear stopped. It

settled down for a meal. Slowly, carefully, hardly breathing, Ron groped for his rifle. He was sweating hard, even though the air was cool. Ron thought: I have no choice. It has to be him or me.

Ron brought the rifle to his shoulder. He found himself trembling. No buck fever now, he told himself. Please, no buck fever. Ron closed his left eye. One shot had to do it.

CHAPTER 4

A River, a Creek, a Storm

The crack of the 30-30 rifle split the stillness. Ron's aim was true. His shot hit the grizzly in the neck. It fell in a heap over the moose carcass.

Ron waited. The grizzly was down, but was it dead? There's only one thing more dangerous than a grizzly. And that is a wounded grizzly. Some people have plunged into the brush after a wounded bear, only to find too late that they had made a mistake. So Ron waited.

The light grew dim. The crumpled bear still had not moved. But Ron had to be sure. He had to know before complete darkness came on.

Cautiously he approached the animal. Ron hated to use another shot, for his ammunition was running low. Who could tell when he might reach help? But he could take no chances. Ron fired a second shot into the grizzly. Then, satisfied, he went back and crawled into his sleeping bag.

On the fourteenth day Ron Woodcock came to a wide river. He didn't think he could swim it and still keep his food and equipment. And the river looked too deep for him to wade across.

So Ron swung off to the west. He spent all day traveling in that direction. Near sundown he came to a stream. It was too wide to leap across. And the water flowed too wildly for Ron to risk wading. So he thought of another solution. He would try to make a bridge.

He set his backpack down and took out his ax. Then, choosing a tree on the edge of the stream, Ron started to chop. His swift, clean strokes drove the ax ever deeper into the tree. Then, just as it started to fall, Ron dropped his ax and pushed on the tree, trying to guide it.

With a crash the tree fell into the stream. But the water ran too swiftly. It swept the tree away as though it were a toothpick.

Ron chose another tree. Again he swung his ax. Again the tree went down. And again the same thing happened.

Fighting the brush all day had tired Ron. Now felling two trees had exhausted him. He could do no more hard work right then. He camped, chewed a few pieces of moose meat and a little rice, and went to sleep.

The next morning Ron took stock. The river blocked his route to the south. The stream, run-

ning into the river, blocked him from the west. There was only one thing to do, he decided. He would have to turn north. Perhaps he could find a place on the stream narrow enough for him to cross. And so, with the sun on his right, Ron set out. He found no crossing point that day.

Late in the afternoon of that fifteenth day, huge storm clouds began to form in the western sky. Studying them, Ron knew he was in for a wet night.

He camped in a grove of spruce trees. And before he did anything else, Ron went to work with his ax. One after another he felled young spruce trees. He piled them up to form a shelter. Then he felled more and dragged them inside.

The soft spruce leaves would make a good mattress. And they would keep Ron off the ground and less wet.

The storm struck just as darkness fell. It was a fierce blow, with heavy winds and pelting, slashing rain. From around him Ron could hear trees crashing to the ground, brought down by the high wind.

All night and all the next day the storm raged. Ron stayed huddled in his sleeping bag. There was nowhere to go. He had plenty of time to think.

He thought about Bill Jenkins, the bush pilot. He wondered what Jenkins would think when he found no one waiting for him at the cabin on Lake Damochax. But what Ron thought about most was his family. What were his wife and kids doing now? he wondered. Most of all he thought: will I ever see them again?

CHAPTER 5

A Search

Early in June, Bill Jenkins looked over his calendar. In two days he would have to fly to Lake Damochax to pick up Ron Woodcock.

The day Jenkins left was fine—sunny, with only a few clouds in the sky. He took off smoothly from Lake Fraser and headed northwest.

Jenkins reached Lake Damochax and landed about noon. He taxied the plane toward the cabin. But Jenkins saw no one, and no smoke came from the chimney. He was puzzled. Did he have the wrong day? He checked. No, he thought, the day is right. But that's about the only thing that is. Jenkins had expected Ron to be there waiting. Loaded with beaver skins, Ron would have been more than eager to be off for home after eight weeks in the wilderness.

Cutting his engine, Jenkins dropped anchor into the shallow water and waded ashore. He went up to the cabin and entered it. A few beaver traps were there, nothing more. It looked as though no one had been there for many days.

Now Jenkins began to worry. What had happened? Had Ron lost track of the days? Did something go wrong? Should he search? Jenkins had no food with him, so he couldn't stay long in the wilderness. To remain longer would be a waste of time. The best thing was to return right away to Endako and get help.

Back in Endako, Jenkins found Ron's brother

and his brother-in-law. He gave them the news—no Ron. He also talked with Ron's wife.

They were all for starting right away. But Jenkins stopped them. They could get to Lake Damochax before sunset, but that would leave little time to search that day. Better wait until morning and be off at dawn. Everyone finally agreed to that, but Ron Woodcock's wife didn't sleep that night.

The next day, as the first rays of the sun struck Lake Fraser, the three men took off. And when they arrived at Lake Damochax, Jenkins could see that nothing had changed. The cabin still stood empty and silent.

For four days the men searched, along creeks and into the wilderness. They found nothing, no sign that any human had been around. Then, late in the afternoon of the fourth day, they came across something they had missed. At the point where a creek flows into the lake, the men found a raft made of logs. It lay there overturned.

Had Ron made that raft to float beaver skins down the creek? And had it turned over, perhaps in a storm? Had Ron drowned? All that could have happened.

Anyway, the three men had found no other sign. They decided that Ron indeed was dead. There was nothing more they could do. They

returned to Endako to tell Ron's wife that she was now a widow. She had to tell the children that they no longer had a father.

CHAPTER 6

A Long Walk Ends

By the morning of the seventeenth day, the storm had passed. Still completely lost but very much alive, Ron dried himself and his belongings. He then headed north again along the stream. He still hoped to find a place to cross.

And he found one. Now safely on the west bank of the stream, Ron turned south again. Much time had been lost. But, he said to himself, "Take it easy. You'll get out."

By the twenty-fifth day, the last of Ron's food was gone. So he looked for plants to eat. He remembered that he had once seen cows munching parts of the Solomon's Seal plant. They must be safe to eat, he thought, and he tried them. Moose like squawberries, he knew. He found some. They were sour and made his mouth pucker, but they gave him a little strength. Ron had lost weight, he figured about twenty pounds.

Then, hacking through the underbrush one

morning, he came upon a most welcome sign. There, rotting on the ground, lay an old telegraph pole. Ron knew that he had come across a telegraph line that had been built nearly a hundred years before. If he could just find signs of a trail, it might lead to Hazelton.

Ron cut himself a walking stick. He sharpened one end. As he moved, he pushed the stick into the ground. If the ground was hard, he was on the trail over which many men and animals had passed. If the ground was soft, he was off the trail. He had to feel his way back to it.

But by now Ron Woodcock could hardly push one foot ahead of the other. His body was gradually giving out. He sometimes lost the trail in thick growths of moss, trees, and brush. Sometimes he came to swamp. He had to circle around it. Thick growths of willow trees also forced him to detour. He lost the trail whenever he did so. Then he had to zig and zag, back and forth, until he found it again. During two weeks he figured he moved no more than twenty miles toward his goal, Hazelton. How much longer? he thought. Will I last?

The forty-third day. Ron had eaten nothing but leaves and wild berries for three weeks. His strength was almost gone. He moved his belt down to the last notch. But by this time he had become so skinny the belt wouldn't hold his pants

up. He took the strap off his rifle and made a suspender of it.

Now the sole of one his boots flapped loosely. Ron found a piece of string in his pack and tied the sole to the upper part of the boot.

Sharp bushes tore his clothing. He couldn't mend the rips.

Mosquitoes swarmed about him, all the time it seemed. His forehead grew raw and bloody from their bites.

All Ron could find to eat now were bush cranberries. They have large seeds. The seeds gave Ron terrible cramps. He could hardly stand up. Still, he forced his rubbery legs to drag him along, step after painful step. He had to make it, he told himself. He had to.

On the fiftieth day, Ron couldn't get up. He knew that somewhere ahead was the road to Hazelton. But his strength was gone. "Is this the end?" he asked. "Rest awhile," he told himself, panting hard. He no longer thought of lost beaver, or even of his family. All Ron could think about was how tired he was.

At last, pushing hard on his walking stick, Ron heaved himself to his feet. He stumbled forward. He squinted to focus his eyes. Saliva lay thick in his mouth and throat. It was hard to breathe. Two more days, he thought. Only two more days. I can't last a third day.

44

Yet somehow he did. At about noon on the fifty-seventh day, Ron stumbled onto a dirt road—the road to Hazelton. Only his walking stick held him up. He weaved back and forth, almost falling. He wanted to cheer, but he couldn't.

Squinting down the road, Ron spotted a car coming. As it passed him, the two men in it stared at what seemed to be a scarecrow beside the road. Make them stop, Ron begged. Make them stop!

About a hundred and fifty feet past Ron, the car halted. It backed up. Painfully, Ron staggered toward the car as the two men got out.

He needed water badly. But he couldn't talk. He made a motion like writing and one of the men gave him a pad and pencil. Slowly moving his hand, Ron wrote: "I need water." One of the men reached into the car and brought out a bottle. Ron forced himself to drink. Then he wrote: "Please take me to my mother's house in Hazelton."

As the men helped Ron into the back seat, he leaned against the cushion and thought: I made it. I beat the wilderness. I made it.

Ron's mother didn't recognize him. He had a heavy beard. His weight was down to about 100 pounds. His arms and legs were like sticks. His clothing was tattered and torn. Ron collapsed.

For two weeks Ron Woodcock lay in a hospital. During the first three days he couldn't talk above a whisper. After leaving the hospital, he spent two more months getting his health and strength back.

Many people later asked Ron about his lonely trek through the wilderness. He tried to tell them how it had been, how he had felt. But for a long time, whenever he did he cried. He couldn't help himself. He had had a great adventure. It was his only, something that was difficult to share with others. He alone had passed what must have been the hardest test any human could be put to. Ron Woodcock had met the worst the wilderness had to offer. And he had survived.